T0128245

Here I Am, Lord. Send Me

One Man's Spiritual Journey

Fain McKinney

WESTBOW
PRESS®
A DIVISION OF THOMAS NELSON
& ZONDERVAN

WestBow Press books may be ordered through booksellers or by contacting:

WestBow Press
A Division of Thomas Nelson & Zondervan
1663 Liberty Drive
Bloomington, IN 47403
www.westbowpress.com
1 (866) 928-1240

ISBN: 978-1-9736-3140-8 (sc)
ISBN: 978-1-9736-3141-5 (hc)
ISBN: 978-1-9736-3139-2 (e)

Library of Congress Control Number: 2018907786

Print information available on the last page.

WestBow Press rev. date: 7/5/2018

Contents

Acknowledgments

First, I give thanks to God for giving me the strength and wisdom to be a light for others. And to my Lord and Savior, Jesus Christ, and the Holy Spirit for keeping me.

To my mother, the late Annie Ruth Tymes, thank you for sharing your wisdom and love.

To my grandmother, Lela Porter Tymes, thank you for having faith in me and reminding me that my day would come.

To my Uncle Sonny, who shared his World War II stories of Germany and Korea.

To my wife, thank you for your encouragement, feedback, and editing of this book. I couldn't have done this without you. I love you

To my older sister Marie, thank you for helping me remember the past.

To my beloved, late older brother Melvin, who encouraged me to become a man of integrity.

Finally, thank you to all my brothers and sisters in Christ who supported me through the years and encouraged me to carry the Christian banner: the late Pastor A. B. Duncan, Bishop Harrison Hale, Church of God in Christ Guatemala, World Christianship Ministries, Winning Souls for Christ, Inc, the late Bishop Lucy M Smith PhD., The National Association of Christian Ministers, Catholic Health Services.

Introduction

I believe in the Lord, Jesus Christ, and the Holy Spirit, which both belong to the Trinity of God. The Three in One, the saints and angels that protect us—those that are in Christ Jesus, who is the head of the church that is in his heart, which is open for mankind to inherit within himself.

So many of us feel that life owes us something, but that is so far from the truth. We are in debt to this life we so cherish. If you have been through the first life and know in your heart that you have met our Savior, Jesus Christ, at that crossroad, then you have been given a second chance. All the promises of God, through his son, are now yours.

My life has been better than anything I could have imagined. Everything I have ever wanted, the Lord has provided. I never asked to be rich or famous. I just wanted to love and be loved, work

hard, and treat everyone right. I have always prayed for others, putting them before myself. A friend and brother in God once told me that nobody ever said life would be easy. He was correct.

No matter what life throws your way, flow with it like the wind and go with it. If you learn to accept longsuffering, the end of that situation will result in pure victory within yourself. Don't try to impress humankind or seek worldly reward. God will give you a reward that will lift you up like nothing you could imagine. Only you can try to describe it. Brothers and sisters in the Lord will understand your experience. It's the spiritual inheritance rebirth connection Jesus has given us to be one in each other and with the Father, through him. Hallelujah!

Chapter 1
If Walls Could Talk

As a little boy growing up, I heard sounds that came through the walls of my apartment building. Sounds echoed through the walls of the apartments over us, under us, to the left, and to the right. Sounds of music, making love, arguing, or just plain conversations. Wow! If walls could talk. There are walls around us, and if you just listen, you'll probably hear your own thoughts bouncing back at you.

I can remember hearing when someone got a whipping. And my yells were shouted out across those walls on more than one occasion. If walls could talk, they would recall a lot about you, and you would have to laugh because there were some weird things happening then. Even now, if you live in a project or in an attached home or condo, you

hear some of your neighbors' business for free—and yours too. Many times it has been a blessing for someone to hear through the wall—a person in need of help. In that case, listening to the walls can save a life. If only walls could talk.

I was born in Brooklyn, New York, and lived with three sisters and my mother. I was only four years of age when I came to the realization that I was no longer the little man of the apartment. My mother's new husband had arrived. It took a while for me to accept that I was no longer the only male. Still, I held my peace. Pushing back tears, I told myself that we'd get along just fine.

Growing up on Siegel Street was a somewhat happy time. I was the only male in the apartment, and boy, I was spoiled on more than one occasion by my mother and sisters. There were spankings and then rewards at times. I used to smell the scent of horses in a stable down the street. There were horses and ponies. My mother had a picture taken of me dressed as the Lone Ranger on a white pony; I was wearing a white cowboy hat and silver-handled pistols as I sat upon that pony.

Our community was multicultural. There were Jewish, Italian, and Irish people, as well as

African Americans. Our landlord owned a fish market downstairs as part of the building. He was a nice man, and we had fish every Friday night. Some things I remember as if they were yesterday. I remember the smell of coal in the cast-iron stove.

Then there were the holidays, like Easter, Halloween, and Christmas. Each holiday was filled with its own special memories. On Easter, I looked forward to the Easter egg hunt. We didn't have friends. People like my family stayed to themselves. On Halloween, my mother use to scare us with a story of a boogieman who would come after us if we were to move from the bed. She would place a glass of water under the bed for the boogieman. My sisters and I were terrified. If we had to go to the bathroom, it was done in the bed. We were not leaving the bed. Not to mention the gorilla man who my mother would have come by to scare us kids half to death. Christmas was somewhat sad for me because while other children got clothes and toys as gifts, we got maybe a piece of fruit and a shirt, socks, or undergarments, but no toys. So Christmas wasn't my favorite holiday.

Children used to boast of all the gifts they received. They laughed and talked about us having none and how their parents gave my mother

shoes for me. I can still remember the pair of Buster Brown shoes I had with a hole in the sole. I was taught to place folded newspaper in the shoes so I could wear them in the rain and snow.

My mother raised us to be humble and to be thankful that we were alive. I had become so used to being humiliated that when I learned a little about Jesus and how the Jewish people in the Old Testament survived, it didn't bother me to an extent. Growing up to be Fain wasn't easy.

My Name Is Champ

I'd like to let you know that life is something to appreciate once you've lived long enough to understand its perspective. I was blessed to have been given a big brother who loved me more than life itself. I was nine years old when I was introduced to my older brother. After learning that I had a big brother, I was so excited and filled with anxious expectations of a hero; he was someone I could boast about to my peers—and to my enemies.

You see, I was considered a nerd, so to speak. I was an odd kind of child. I mostly kept to myself, and I didn't follow others. I was taught to stay away

from following other boys and doing bad things, such as being ill-mannered. I just couldn't do wrong. Other boys mocked me and tried bullying me.

Occasionally, I had to show one or two—and sometimes three at a time—that I was not afraid. Even though my heart raced and my legs trembled from fear, I stood my ground. I didn't run. I couldn't, for the sake of my life, understand why I didn't run as fast as fallen leaves blown by the wind. I stood my ground and took the first blow to my jaw, and then it was on.

So many times, I had to fight for my life. Well, I am glad I didn't run because the next day my adversary and I would make up, and we'd be friends for life. So when my big brother came to light, and I saw a giant of a figure—or so he seemed to be to me—I was very happy and felt that now I wouldn't be bullied ever again.

My brother was raised in the south, in rural Georgia. I had listened to my mother share shocking stories from her childhood of white men dressed in sheets. They were treated like slaves. Some of the things I learned about the treatment of my family in the south were demeaning and subhuman. I use to cry like Jesus did over Lazarus

when Jesus was told of his death. I felt the pain of death and couldn't do anything about it. I was often comforted by stories of my family going through so many atrocities yet still standing. They didn't run. I learned that my grandfather was a hard worker, and my grandmother was a midwife. They raised many other children who had lost their parents to death—even their grandchildren, like my older brother and sister. I guess that's why I couldn't run from bullies.

When my brother saw me for the first time, I can remember him towering over me, and I looked up to him. He stood six feet tall, which at that time I just knew meant he was a giant. He told me that we were never to fight one another over money or women. I couldn't help but listen to him. Then he stated that in a few more years, he would tell me what type of man I had become. Believe me, I took his statement to heart. I was determined to be the best man I could be.

I had the baddest brother in Brooklyn. He was well respected. Because of my being the baby boy of the family—which included my oldest sister, my brother, my sister who half mothered me, me, and then two younger sisters—I was sort of spoiled but was also pushed around by them all. When there

was a sibling battle, I would pass messages between them until they reconciled their differences.

Throughout my childhood, I had to keep thinking about not being a weak-minded kid. I had to accept the daily peer pressure of being mocked about having a stepdad who drank. It made me feel embarrassed and ashamed to call him my dad. I was being picked on to fight and couldn't because my mother would tell me not to fight and instead to let God fight my battles.

This was not always the case. Eventually, I had to learn to hit back because I could always hear my older brother's voice telling me that I shouldn't be a wimp. I was sort of confused and angry. I had begun to store up anger because I was told not to be a fighter, a wimp, and especially a pimp. Yes, a pimp: someone who makes others use their bodies for the sole purpose of selling themselves sexually to earn an income for another. I could never be a pimp, even though those guys drove the finest cars and wore the most dashing shoes and clothing in the world. Therefore, I had to dream of becoming something else. It would take a few more years to determine exactly what that would be.

Chapter 2

Crossroads

From time to time, tragic things can happen that can impact you so hard that you believe that you cannot live any longer. I was at such a crossroads at the age of fourteen, when I found out that my mother had succumbed to liver disease and other complications.

It was early on a Saturday morning, and my mother had given me the okay to go out to play alone because she knew that there were no other boys outside that early to bully me or get me into trouble. But this Saturday morning was totally the opposite. A couple of boys were outside, and they were up to no good. They were riding bikes. One of the bikes was a purple Vroom bike that had a banana-saddle seat with high handlebars and chrome wheels and fenders. Wow!

They approached and made me an offer I couldn't refuse. They offered me that bike under the terms that if I would ride on the back of the mini bike with one of them to go to Manhattan to steal a bike, I could have that Vroom bike. I was in trouble now. One of my mother's and one of God's commandments was now about to be broken. I tell you no lie: I was at my first crossroad I had ever experienced.

I could feel the devil on my left shoulder whispering in my ear, "Don't worry. Your mother won't find out." And an angel on my right shoulder was warning me what would happen when my mother got her hands on me for doing it. My mother would kill me.

Well, the devil won that day because he told me, "Hey, you always wanted a bike, and you know your parents can't afford it. Go ahead, and if you make it back, you will have the bike of your dreams." My choice was made. I decided to listen to the devil. I remember that ride on the back of that bike: every pothole that pounded my little butt as we rode the Brooklyn Bridge from Bedford-Stuyvesant to Manhattan. My heart pounded with fear. I remember riding through Delancey Street where everyone went to buy the best clothes: all the well-known brands that I wished I could have had.

There we were, like sharks looking for smaller fish to eat, but this was for a bike. Comparing the taking of a bike to a shark stalking smaller fish is not too much different. He must kill his prey, and stealing someone's bike could lead to maybe killing someone. The thought of breaking the law was in full bloom. I could go to jail, or I could be killed. I was far from home and had to stay the course to keep from being called a coward or weak if I turned back. So, I was in for the kill or take.

There he was: a single kid on a bike. One of the guys took the bike, and then we were riding for our lives. I was on the bike I always wanted, being chased by two or three bikers. I rode that bike like a stuntman in some James Bond adventure movie. I was dodging in an out of traffic, moving between vehicles as a guy with a chain tried to hit me. By the grace of God, I ducked each time the chain came near my skull. I could hear the *whoosh* sound, and the biker cussing at me to stop. I was never going to stop or die on that day because I knew I just couldn't.

After what seemed like forever, I was back in Brooklyn. As I approached the projects, I noticed an ambulance arriving. I sat on my new bike and watched in shock as my mother was being loaded

in the ambulance. My stepfather joined her. I asked where they were taking my mother. As the ambulance closed the rear door and the driver was given the *go* signal, the sirens blared and the vehicle drove away. I got on my Vroom bike and tried to follow. I remember pedaling as fast as I had when I had stolen the bike, and they were after me.

I made it to the hospital but wasn't allowed on the patient's floor because of my age. Back in the '60s, children had to be fourteen and escorted by an adult to be on patient floors to visit. I took the stairs to avoid security and found my mother's room.

When I arrived, my family, older aunts, uncles, and my mother's sister and brothers were all looking sad and tearing somewhat. I looked at my mother lying in bed with needles in her veins from her feet to head. She was in a coma, and it was uncertain if she would ever awaken. Immediately I grasped her hand in mine and began to pray that God would not take my mother. I heard my sister say, "Momma can't hear you."

At that moment, she mumbled something, and my subconscious heard her saying to remember the things that she had told me before this time had come: not to cry, keep living, and don't die. These

were some of her commandments to me, along with, "Never mistreat someone's daughter because you have a mother and a sister too." That Saturday was the last day of my life. I thought to myself that I would never steal again. As for the bike, I had to let it go because I couldn't keep it in our small apartment, and it really wasn't mine anyhow.

Two days later, upon returning from school, kids told me my mother had passed. I thought they were lying until my stepfather confirmed it. I still refused to believe it. I didn't want to accept that she was never going to be there at home sitting in her kitchen window, surrounded by the flowers she planted.

The aroma of her cooking filled the hallway of the third floor and greeted everyone when they stepped off the elevator. It was that same night that all the family came together to drink, play music, and talk about my mom. She liked to entertain guests. They shared memories of people who she had helped relocate from the south to the north. That was a Saturday to remember because that was the night I decided to end my life. I remember drinking vodka mixed with beer and Bacardi and going to my bedroom. I closed the door to be alone and contemplated leaping from my bedroom window.

My older brother interrupted my plans. He followed me into the bedroom and told me that my mother wouldn't have wanted me to die. I cried that night until I blacked out. That was just the beginning of a test of faith that I was about to embark on. Never think that life owes you anything. Believe me: it doesn't. Two weeks later, my stepfather passed away. So now another test of faith bombarded my sinful life. I had to wonder if all this punishment was for stealing a bike. Did I trade my parents' lives for a bike? If I wasn't to blame, who was? I chose to blame God.

Chapter 3
The Dismantling of My Life

I don't know if you've ever lost everything you owned, but I can tell you, it's not funny at all. It's another faith-testing situation. You must be strong, having at least as much faith as a mustard seed. But at that time in my life, I didn't know a thing about having faith. I was fourteen and helpless. I couldn't say a word about how I felt about anything concerning my feelings. Back then, children in my family were told to keep our mouths shut, at least when grown people were around.

When I use the word *dismantled*, I mean everything from watching all my parents' belongings as well as everything my two sisters and I owned being taken away. Our toys, bed, and furnishings were just gone. I felt that feeling of, *What's going to*

happen to us now? That was just the beginning of what was to come.

The next thing was to find my sister and myself a place to call home. We were about to get the shock of our lives again. First, it was the death of our parents; and then we were separated from one another. We were about to be placed in different homes. Just to let you know a little about my two sisters and myself, we grew up in a somewhat happy but terrifyingly dysfunctional family setting. Our mother was married and had three children by her first husband. I wasn't thought of during those fifteen years before I came along. There was an older sister, older brother, and another sister before me. Then my mother had an extra-marital relationship with a gentleman and gave birth to me and my sister. Finally, my mom got married again to my stepdad and gave birth to a little girl, our baby sister.

During this time, my mother became a totally different person. I could remember few happy times when I smiled. That was whenever my mother was in a good mood when she called us to dinner. My mother was having a very tough time dealing with the loss of her first husband, who was the love of her life. They were married very young and had left the cotton fields of Georgia and the swamps of Florida.

My older sister told me that my mother was fourteen and her father was nineteen years of age. They both fled to New York City and resided in the county of Brooklyn, in the Williamsburg sector. They lived on Siegel Street where I was born.

By second grade, we moved away from Siegel Street, to the projects. I was never around so many people of my own race. It was totally different from what I was used too. Moving into the projects was probably a shock to my mom and stepdad as well. We were used to having everything on our block: fish market, supermarket, night club, barber shop, restaurant, and candy store, all on one block.

For a long period of time, we never went outside except to go to school or visit relatives. My sisters and I were confined to our rooms when we came home from school. We studied, did homework, and played together. There were moments we could look out our room window to watch people as they wandered in and out of the community. There was a large play area made of black tar that was used to play skelly and jump rope or softball, and there were benches to sit on.

My sisters and I could not go outside. Being new to the community, we had to learn to blend into the

environment. My mother knew about the dangers that lurked outside our door. She kept us close to home to keep us safe. We didn't think of it that way, being children. Like most children, we thought our parents were being mean to us when we couldn't do what we wanted to do. We didn't understand that they were really thinking of our safety.

From young childhood to the adolescent age, our minds and brains are still not fully developed to understand our roles in life. We tend to wander in and out of so many unclean decisions about who we are and want to be in life. If you were raised in a rational living environment, you had a better chance to think rational thoughts as you grew into maturity. Others who have been abused in any way may have difficulty thinking rationally when it comes to certain issues concerning their growth into maturity.

If you have been abused in any way, it could affect your decisions and clarity. You could become mentally challenged for the duration of your life unless treated through therapy and other help. Life can be a war zone of the mind, leading to irrational thinking patterns that can lead to thoughts of using alcohol and drugs, anger, low self-esteem, and

possibly suicide. You can become the prey rather than the eagle you were meant to be.

Yes, it's so sad when the abuse we have endured takes over our lives from the early stages of life to adult stages because of a lack of knowledge or prevention. No one ever knew because we were ashamed to let anyone know we were hurt. As for myself, I can identify with those hurts and keeping the pain of abuse to myself over many years from my youth until even now. Writing this book is just one of the ways, after years of suffering, to further the healing process.

As I had mentioned how things began to change after losing my parents, I was sent to live with a relative who had an adopted son. I was seventeen at the time. I felt more abandoned than ever: unloved and abandoned. But I had come to the point of either giving up or making the best decision I could rationalize for myself at this time in my life. I had the choice of becoming that victim of my past or becoming the eagle. I chose the latter and enlisted into the United States Army.

Chapter 4
Basic Training

Earlier, my uncle, a World War II veteran, had shared his story of the war in Germany and Korea, where he had served and became a good man after his life of abuse living in the deep south of Georgia. More than likely, that had a lot to do with my being abused as an African American until today. So that's why I am sharing with you the things I am dealing with, even now, living in America.

When I made the decision to give my life for a nation that never cared for me, or my fathers before me, it was because of my family. This great nation causes abuse to so many of its native and African American families. But thanks be to God, if you have faith the size of a mustard seed and pray, you can overcome your irrational thinking and begin

to fly on the wings of eagles. You can become the person you need to be: a rational thinker.

When I entered the US Army, it was the most challenging experience for a young teenager. Whatever irrational thinking I had before serving in the army, it was completely gone after basic training. There were many who just couldn't make it. They were discharged and left to their own demise. My uncle's love for me kept me alive today. His words were a message of hope. I became a listener and started grasping for life as if I were swimming in deep water and gasping for air to stay alive. I took in all the knowledge of being the best I could be as a young man serving this great nation.

It was during wartime that I joined the army, so it was a good reason to become like an eagle. I passed every training course for combat readiness. I could mop, sweep floors, and make a bed so good and tight that a quarter could bounce off it. I had learned all of this before joining the army.

My mother taught me these things. I can remember the drill sergeant trying to instill discipline in me, and I told him my mother was tougher than him. I was given corporal stripes, and I was given the privilege of training my company barracks

to mop, clean, and make the bunks correctly. My uncle's tales of the army assisted me through everything. If a man couldn't keep up when we marched or ran a mile in six minutes, I would go back and help him complete the march or run. If one man didn't complete our mission or objective, we were all punished. I was a sharpshooter and an expert grenade handler.

I went AWOL during basic training because my baby sister ran away from the family home she was placed with. I received an Article 15 for leaving and missing roll call. I had to report to the captain, but because I told the truth, I was able to accept my punishment. Surprisingly, at graduation, I received my private stripes as a good soldier. I was learning to work on my irrational thinking.

Ambassador of the United States

After leaving advanced infantry training in Fort Gordon, Georgia, I was off to Germany. Following in the footsteps of my uncle, who had been there during World War II, was a dream come true. He told me so much about Germany that I felt like it was home away from the Americas because there, I was homeless. I recollected what my uncle had told

me about Frankfurt, and saw firsthand the 50 caliber bullet holes in buildings that were still standing. I believed my real soldiering would begin now.

Immediately after exiting the plane, I was briefed and told that I was now an ambassador for the United States. Wow! I remember saying to myself, "I am an ambassador!" What a high calling of responsibility. Being black and coming from a poor and suppressed state of unfortunate circumstances, with nobody to call family or friend, I was now an ambassador of the United States of America. I felt proud to be in a country that most people I knew could only dream of seeing in a book.

I was ready to serve my country. Stationed in Stuttgart, Germany, with the 472nd signal battalion, I performed duties as a cable lineman. I repaired cable lines and telephones.

Six months later, the ground would be shaken from under me. Somewhere in the Black Forest, my life was about to change. The rain was pouring down hard that night as I stood guard duty in the woods. There was no shade or covering to keep me from being wet, other than the rain gear. I was left at the base of the mountain until a Jeep approached, heading to the top of the mountain.

The driver stopped and asked me to get out of the rain. I got in the Jeep. The driver was from another company. He needed to check a bunker at the top of the mountain. What made me go with him, I do not know. We arrived at the top, and he checked the bunker. Not long after, when we were on our way down the mountain, the rain became unbearable. We couldn't see the road.

The driver was going too fast as he came around a curve and the wall of the mountain disappeared. We were airborne. I could only believe at this time that it was the end. Fear had me paralyzed as I heard whirling tires. My whole life flashed before me and it was short because I hadn't lived that long.

Suddenly, a funny thing happened that I will never forget. A vision of a cartoon character, Deputy Dog, came into my mind, and I began to laugh in spite of my life being ready to end. I was Deputy Dog and the raccoon. I had watched that cartoon many times as a kid. Everything happened in seconds, but to me, it was in slow motion. Just as the cartoon disappeared, I saw we were heading for a tree. I covered my face to protect it from glass and braced my body for impact.

Despite the pain in my neck, right knee, and back, I could remove my seat belt. I limped around the side of the mangled Jeep to help the driver get free before the Jeep could catch fire. When the medics and MPs arrived, I must have been in shock. I was afraid and trembling. All I could think about was that I didn't want to be discharged from the army. I had to complete something in my life.

When I was asked if I was okay, I said yes; I didn't need medical attention. I didn't want to be put out on a medical discharge. I had to make my mother and my uncle proud of me. I felt the whole world was on my shoulders. I could not fail my mission. My staff sergeant was very caring and showed concern for my well-being. He asked if I needed medical attention. Fear answered for me as I refused.

My commander captain asked to see me, and I had to fill out an accident report, and I had to go on medical leave. I had only one place back in the States that I could try to go, and that was to my older sister. There I was, on a plane back to the States. This was around the end of November 1971, just a week before my birthday in December. My sister and her husband at the time greeted me with open arms when I arrived at their door. I was back in the States. It felt like fear had won.

Chapter 5

A Self-Made Hero

After thirty days of being stateside, I received new orders to report to Korea. I was shocked by the sudden transfer from Germany to Korea. I didn't realize that I was fulfilling a lifetime dream that became a reality. When my uncle was telling me of his World War II journey, neither one of us could have ever known that God was at work, making preparations for me. After a brief stop in Alaska for refueling, it was on to Tokyo, Japan, and, from there, Korea.

Landing in Korea was really a scary feeling for me. Although I had been told about Korea, being there at last, breathing the air, was chilling and exciting. There at the airport was my new company transport vehicle waiting to take me to Camp Casey

2nd Division Battalion. I now belonged to the 122nd Signal Battalion.

After being introduced to my company, I stayed on base for six months before I had the nerve to go into the village. I had spent time working on assignments as a cable lineman. I finally had the nerve to leave the base. I can remember that first night in Tong do Chan. There were door-to-door night clubs everywhere. It seemed endless. Loud music, alcohol, and plenty of Korean women. I was shocked at so many beautiful Korean women coming and asking skinny old me for a night in bed. I was warned about this happening during processing into the country and orientation class. There were instructions on how to be an ambassador and a soldier representing the United States. The lecture also warned us of the possible sexual diseases and precautions we could take to keep from being a victim of casual sex, which would result in trips to the medics for injections in the rear end.

That first night, after a visit to several clubs on the north side of the village, we wandered over to the south side, and it was there where I finally found a reason to want to come back to the village. At this one club, a waitress served our table. After we made eye contact, I was feeling something like romance,

like cupid had shot an arrow into my heart. I sat there, not in a lustful state. I was not looking for any sexual relationship because I was afraid of getting an STD. I really wanted to get to know her for more than a sexual relationship. I felt like she was the woman I had always dreamt of, and I had to meet her.

Later that night, just before closing time, which was two o' clock in the morning, a soldier came in and went over to the waitress and began arguing with her. He hit her in the face and walked out of the club. I was feeling no pain, and I proceeded out of the club to become involved in that situation. I couldn't help but get involved. My mind and body went into a self-made hero mode that I created from watching heroes on television like the Lone Ranger, Tarzan, and *Have Gun, Will Travel*. There are so many. As a child, I had wanted to be a hero. Something brings it out of me, and I'm on my mission to rescue whoever needs rescuing.

After chasing after that soldier, I caught up to him before he could jump into the taxi and flee. I stopped the taxi and opened the back door. I had no feelings of fear, only of making him pay for his actions. I asked him why he struck the Korean woman. He said he was her boyfriend and wanted

to know why I was angry with him. He said she was only Korean, as if to say she meant nothing to him and that I shouldn't be concerned about what happened to her because of her race. But I told him that he shouldn't have hit her because I cared.

I explained to him that if a man had hit his mother or sister, how would he feel and what would his response be? He apologized. At that time, I heard people applauding and thanking me for what I had done. An audience of Koreans came over to the taxi. They seemed shocked to see a soldier defending one of them. I shut the taxi door, and that soldier knew I may have saved his life also. I didn't feel so much a hero at that time, only that I had done the right thing.

I went back to the club to check on the waitress. I inquired as to her whereabouts and was directed upstairs to her room. After a minute or two, I left my shoes outside the room and entered. She was nursing a bruised eye. I gave her a smile and shared my concern for her recovery. I told her that if I could help in any way, I would be there. The time had come to return to the base.

I knew I had to catch that deuce and half truck from my company before it left me behind. My

company was a long way from the main gate. So I asked to return on another day when I had leave to come to the village again.

From that time on, we got to know each other as friends. I didn't impose on her for sex. I wanted to be her boyfriend and husband if that was at all possible. I was eighteen years old and in love. She had a wonderful personality. She was older than me and had a no-nonsense personality. I made every moment with her special during the twelve months I served in Korea. I wanted to marry her, but I was too young and needed consent to marry at that age. I can say that being in Korea with her made it easier to cope with the hardship of that tour.

I spent many days on the DMZ, putting up telephone lines and feeling a knot in my stomach as we drove across the bridge. We were working on the 3rd parallel line, watching the North Koreans watching us as we climbed those telephone poles with new cable for communications. I was living a dream that had become reality. I shared earlier how my uncle used to tell me about Korea as a child. Well, there I was, in the place where hundreds of lives were lost, and the voice of a woman spoke from a loud speaker telling me to go home; that this was not my war.

I was scared to death of being shot and killed while I stood at the top of those telephone poles, drilling a hole to secure cables after putting my jay hook and pigtail clamps to align the cable. My eyes were constantly moving from my work to the Korean soldiers that watched me. That very thing stays in my head to this day. If I hear a firecracker, I jump to the ground. I am always thinking combat readiness. I don't trust anybody, not even my family. I watch rooftops and windows when I walk through a community. I have no life. I don't enjoy myself at a park or beach, not even my own backyard. I don't sleep. I could never keep a job. I have been homeless for most of my life since leaving the army. Believe me, *life* has been a four-letter word. I didn't know it had another name: PTSD (Post-Traumatic Stress Disorder).

Chapter 6
PTSD and Me

After serving two years of non-civilian life, I was honorably discharged. I was back in the United States without a home to go to. Nobody met me at the airport. I thought to myself, *Where can I find a place to sleep? Where can I find a job? Who is going to let me stay at their home?* I returned to the very place I had run away from: the home of my great uncle, his wife, and their adopted son. This is the very place I left to die on the battlefield. I felt it was better to give my life for my country rather than die of feeling abandoned and alone.

I now had to learn how to fit back into the norm of surviving with civilians. When a soldier comes back home, everything is totally blank to him or her about how to cope with normal, day-to-day living again. All I could think of was having my rifle and

grenades to harm anyone who looked at me the wrong way. At the time, it seemed like there wasn't any job I could handle.

A few weeks after settling in, I looked for work, and to my surprise, I was hired by the US Postal Service. That job was just as trying as being in the army. At least in the army, you knew your company had your back. In civilian life, the supervisors are trained to be your worst enemies. They make you want to quit.

I was a letter carrier/clerk. After leaving the army, I was not in any condition to go right to work for any company of any kind. But who was going to tell me that? I was black, and the US Army didn't care for black soldiers. Although I tried to keep jobs, I was in a battle with myself. I had jobs like the post office, police department, and many off-the-books jobs that paid nothing in cash that I couldn't blow in alcohol and drugs. I was more comfortable being homeless, without a care in the world, than having a decent home and a job.

I found myself feeling I had no reason to live, so I continually keep myself in a disastrous position in my life. This caused me relationship issues with others. I had become jobless on several occasions.

I was divorced three times. I married one woman twice, not to mention the several other women I was with who evicted me. I had nothing to live for. I even forgot that I was the father of three sons. I had gone over the edge and stumbled into the world of crack cocaine.

I have tried every drug from hash, acid, joints, wine, and more. I went from cocaine powder to cooking it into rocks and then taking that fast kick, to only wanting another as long as a dollar was in my hands. Sleeping in the parks, streets, and abandoned buildings was all good. Then it was back to the crack. I had an apartment that I was shacking up at with a wonderful woman, and I walked away to chase the crack. I left everything I owned: two cars, all my nice clothing, jewelry, and work clothes.

I was a security officer and was injured on the job due to a mental patient. I was taken into the emergency room and left there for hours before being seen. I realized then that the job wasn't for me. I was a professional doing security after leaving the service. I did work for several big security companies. I worked in the jewelry sector, private sector, and in malls. But all the time, I was learning that working for certain companies can make you feel worthless.

Crack-Cocaine Journey

I am a living witness to the fact that God is good. I have lived through so many of the things that you have read in my story, and even now as I write, I am so inspired by the Word of God that it has become a living fire in my soul. Now, I will share my story of meeting my true Father. He is the very one who helped me endure every trial and tribulation while I was doing everything that I wanted and thinking I had control of my own life. Finally, when I had come to the very point in my life when death could have been the final road, I AM showed up. Yes, God himself or his Angel.

I had given in to believing that there had to be a higher power, and I was not alone anymore. This is how I came into the faith of Christianity. After living in the world of alcohol and drugs that had me believing that I was in the glorious fame of reality, I thought that all that glittered was gold. The glitter of that feeling of being high was all that mattered to me.

That feeling of not having a problem in the world had taken me for a ride every time I lit up a cigarette, smoked a joint, or drank alcohol. But that wasn't enough. I had to try the ultimate drug called

crack. I can tell you that after the first flick of the lighter and the sound of the *snap, sizzle,* and *pop,* you are on your way to the continued chase of wanting another episode: that same flick of the lighter and sound of crack sizzling in that hot steam.

I had come to that moment in my life when I just didn't care anymore. I had lived a life of abandonment. I was unable to find love no matter how hard I tried to show my love for my country or other people. But the words my mother and grandmother taught me were stuck in my head. I was to show love to everyone, no matter what came from them. I took whatever people dished at me and showed love to them in return.

I can remember when I was out on those streets doing those self-inflicting things, using drugs. Many times, I would give my last to anyone who needed it. I used to stand in the soup lines at churches, and the feeling of being on the other side of the handout would fill my heart with compassion for others. If I received an apple or orange, I would put it in my pocket for someone else who was hungry. Nevertheless, I continued my self-pity trip I had taken as my excuse for getting high.

It took ten years of suffering in my self-pity and excuses before I realized what I had missed out on in my life. I was at death's door. I had no idea what I looked like because I stayed away from looking in a mirror. I slept during the day and prowled the streets at night. I was living like a rodent, only coming out at night to eat and get high. I came in during the day only to run to the crack line at the house where the crack was sold. The abandoned building and crack dens where people could go to get high were where I could be found. I was going to die a slow death. I had no knowledge of how to cry out for help nor was help going to come to me. At least that's what I thought.

Just before the day that help would come, I was shocked by the arrival of my sons. Yes, my sons who I hadn't seen since they were able to walk came into the abandoned building that I was living in. I will always remember seeing them walking down the long hallway of the building. I could only see two figures coming toward me. As they approached me, I began thinking about being absent from their lives for so many years. I wondered, *Are they coming to kill me?*

I was speechless as they stood in front of me. They suddenly said, "Dad, we love you. What are

you doing to yourself? You are all we have now that our mother has died. You are all we have." I felt so hopeless and unworthy of those words, "We love you." That was a day I will forever remember. I didn't abandon my sons. Their mother left me after a fire in the building where we lived. The building was unlivable, so their mother gave them to her mother through adoption and moved on with her life. I used to visit them but was told not to come to see them.

The grandmother didn't want them to be disappointed by me not having a job and making promises I couldn't keep. That was another excuse for me to continue getting high. After my sons stayed with me for a while that day, they left, and my older sister showed up. She told me to find a mirror and look into it to see myself looking like I was near death.

I found a mirror, and when I glanced into it, I saw the face of death looking back. I was confused and shocked that I had brought myself to this point in my life. I saw my facial features were like the skeleton of a dead man. My skin tone had become so dark that I couldn't believe that figure in the mirror was me. I can remember feeling a sense of fear and what I recognized now to be anxiety. I had become very frightened by wanting another hit of crack. I

was exhausted and out of my mind. B*ut what do I do?* Asking for help was too far away from my mind to comprehend. But as I was trembling with fear for my life, I knew I wanted help.

I didn't know how to pray or plead for my life to the Christian faith. I had been a fool. I had lied to God, who I didn't know. Over and over, I had cried out to God to help me when I was going through nights where my head was spinning out of whack from overindulgence in alcohol and crack. I would call on God to help me, saying, "God, if you take this feeling from me, I promise not to indulge ever again." Who was I fooling? Nobody but myself. Lie after lie I told God. But this was a time when I really needed to ask him for help. I had become so withdrawn from believing he would answer me if I called upon him to help me, so I didn't ask him. I am saying *him* because I was taught to perceive him as a male figure. If only I could pray or scream out to somebody to tell him I needed help.

The following morning, to my surprise, I was met by a brother-in-law who came to take me to a medical center for veterans. I didn't think twice when he offered to take me to see if I could be helped. I said yes, and was given the privilege to regain some of my life. I felt so sincere within my

soul and started to believe I could be the man I had wanted to be when I was a child. I was on my way to becoming alive again. The chance of a lifetime had come my way to let my sons see their dad become a positive role model. I had to prove to myself that I could achieve anything I put my mind to.

Chapter 7
Me, Myself, and I AM

I was transferred to a hospital for two weeks for observation and then to a shelter for veterans. While at the shelter, I received rehabilitation. I also received training to achieve a certificate as a Human Services Assistant. It was fifteen months well spent, and I began to volunteer at the shelter to help anyone who needed help. During my time at the shelter, my spirit of self-worth grew more than I ever imagined.

To my surprise, I was about to meet my real Father. God would use another homeless veteran to lead the way and draw me to himself. This veteran slept opposite of my bunk, and he was always reading the Holy Bible. For days and nights, I would watch him reading until one day I just had to ask

him to help me understand what was inspiring him to read the Bible.

He shared his testimony of using the same drug I had used: crack cocaine. He had lost everything. When he showed me pictures of those he had lost, I felt so bad. Then he began to show me the Holy Bible. When he shared some of the things about Jesus and Paul's journey, I became amused and wanted to know more.

He had so much knowledge of their journey from one place to the other, and he knew the distances they walked too. I was overwhelmed by his faith. That young man stated he was going to have his family back and more than what he lost. Once again, I believed him. What a surprise. I asked for his help to show me how I could become knowledgeable about the Bible and receive like-minded faith to believe the same things were possible for me. He told me to come to Bible and prayer service at the shelter on Thursday nights.

For several nights, I started attending those services, and then one night as I was leaving the meeting to return to my bunk, I heard a voice say to me, "You can come to me now or return to the way you were." I stopped and shook my head as if I

were hearing something, but I didn't believe it was for me.

The voice spoke again with these same words, and immediately my thoughts turned to Moses and Samuel. God's voice spoke to them too. Immediately, I threw my hands up and stated, "Lord, if you take me back, I promise I will never leave you." I heard myself say that to God.

The same God I denied knowing and had lied to repeatedly, I was now surrendering my life to. I could feel a sincerity in myself that I had never felt before. That night and for many nights, I would battle with my sinful self in my dreams and actions. I had the power to defeat those dreams of sexual desires and accepting drinks or drugs in my sleep.

The devil couldn't touch me again. I would awaken every time Satan showed up, trying to deceive me. I would get on my knees and tarry the name of Jesus repeatedly until I was able to talk to him while I was tarrying.

What a sense of joy and peace and love I had all around me. It was that feeling of the Spirit of God comforting me, saying, "Well done." From that day,

when things came to me to challenge my faith, I could overcome them without fear.

There was an incident at the shelter that I would like to share with you. One veteran was being accused of stealing something from another veteran. I just happened to hear the accusations and saw the crowd wanted to harm him. There I was in the middle of a situation that brought to mind the time Jesus stood up for Mary Magdalene, who was about to be stoned by a mob. Jesus stood before the accusers and dared anyone who hadn't sinned to throw the first stone.

Well, I found myself in that same situation as I watched that crowd wanting to harm that poor lost soul of a man. I shouted out, "If there is any one of us who has not stolen before, then be the first to go through with assaulting that man." At that moment, it became silent, and everyone retreated to whatever they were doing beforehand. At first, I thought they might turn on me, but to my surprise, others came to me and thanked me.

From that day on, they began to call me Reverend. I have never been that afraid since I was a child being asked to come out after school and fight. I would leave school through the back exit

and take the long way home. I believe God tests us to see if we are sincere in our faith to him. My life has changed for the better. I was forty years of age when I received my second chance at life.

I moved into a single residence occupancy in Harlem, New York, and I attended meetings and groups for homeless veterans. Finally, I was introduced into my own apartment in the Bronx. I attended a program that taught me office skills. Seventeen months later, I became a bus driver.

I drove for New York City Transit Authority/ MABSTOA for five years. I had to retire due to health problems that developed after voluntarily driving the firemen to Ground Zero of the World Trade Center site. Thanks be to God that I am able to share my story. I want to thank you for reading my story, and I pray that you will come to know the Great I AM, even as he knows you.

Printed in the United States
By Bookmasters